D0887430

Tees
Felt Fashions

Design and decorate tees that are sure to please!

⭐ American Girl®

Published by American Girl Publishing
Copyright © 2011 American Girl

Questions or comments? Call 1-800-845-0005, visit **americangirl.com**, or write to
Customer Service, American Girl, 8400 Fairway Place, Middleton, WI 53562-0497.

Printed in China
14 15 16 17 18 19 20 LEO 11 10 9 8 7 6 5 4

All American Girl marks are trademarks of American Girl.

Editorial Development: Carrie Anton, Trula Magruder

Art Direction & Design: Camela Decaire

Production: Jeannette Bailey, Sarah Boecher, Tami Kepler, Judith Lary, Trudi Jenny

Photography: Kristin Kurt, Greg Petz

Photography Stylists: Lori Decker, Kim Sphar, Jane Amini

Craft Stylist: Carrie Anton

Craft with Care

When creating crafts or accessories that will touch your doll, remember
that dye colors from ribbons, felt, beads, and other supplies may bleed
color onto a doll and leave permanent stains. To help prevent this, use
light colors when possible, and check your doll often to make sure
colors aren't transferring to her body or vinyl. And never get your doll
wet! Water greatly increases the risk of dye rub-off.

Wash!

wash your designed tees—they will not ___ up to machine or hand washing. If you get ___ stain on an area not near the design, you can ___ ask an adult to help you spot clean it. Avoid sticky fingers, rough play, dirt, and water, and your tee designs will last longer.

Tweezers

Tweezers can help you to position small crafting supplies such as beads, googly eyes, and pom-poms.

Swap It!

Make the most of your designs by creating changeable tee appliqués. Using adhesive hook-and-loop fasteners, attach a hook piece to the the tee and a loop piece to the appliqué. When your doll needs a fresh look, swap one design for another.

Beads & Dimensional Fabric Paint

In this book, appliqué faces are most often made with beads or dimensional fabric paint. When using beads, apply a small amount of craft glue to the bead and then position the bead in place and hold until dry.

When you see this symbol, it means that dimensional fabric paint was used. When using paint, be sure to test the applicator bottle on a piece of scrap paper. Some bottles get air bubbles, which can cause the paint to splatter. Testing also helps you see the thickness and speed at which paint comes out.

Tee Templates

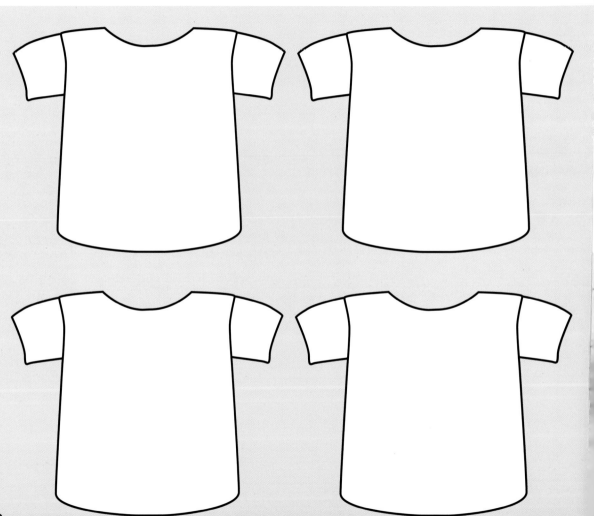

Before you make anything permanent, draw out your designs to see what you think. When you have a plan you like, decorate a tee!

Pet Party

Amazing appliqués to celebrate your love of animals

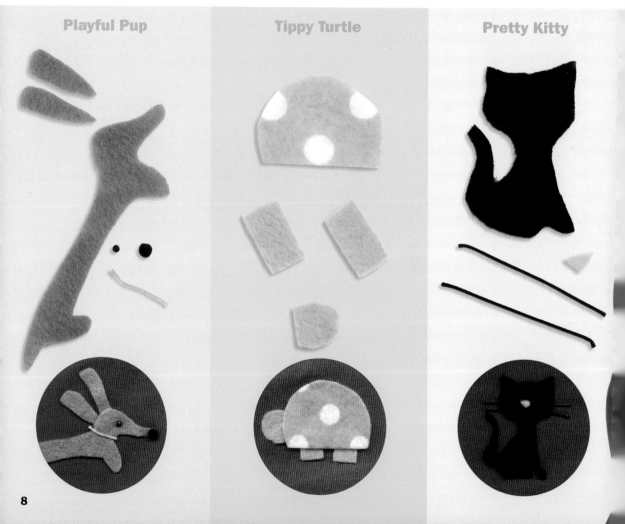

Playful Pup

Tippy Turtle

Pretty Kitty

Sweet Tweets

Fun fashions featuring a flock of feathered friends

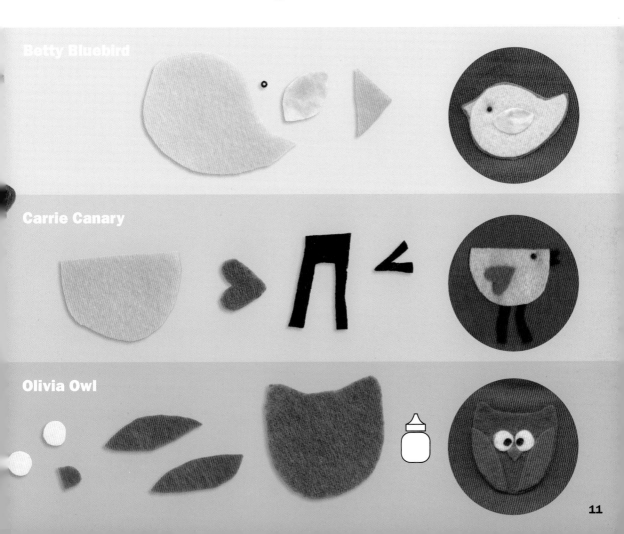

Betty Bluebird

Carrie Canary

Olivia Owl

11

Blooming Branches

Trunks and leaves create terrific tree tees.

Tree Love

Woodsy Wonder

Fall Beauty

Creature Feature

Craft a tee starring these wild things.

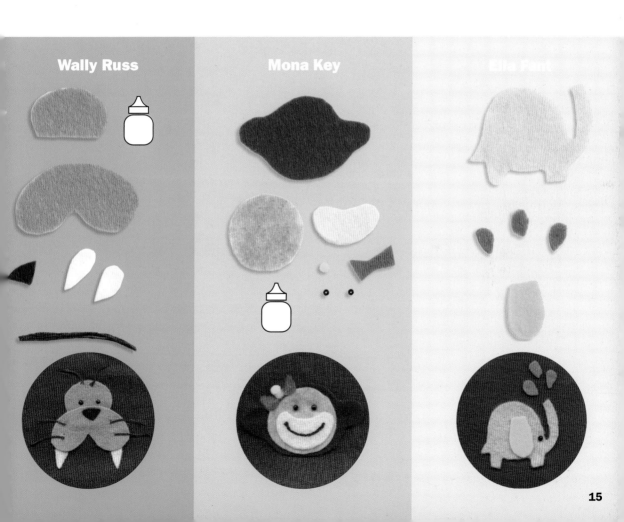

Wally Russ

Mona Key

Ella Fant

Snack Time

Tasty-treat tees show off your doll's sweetness.

Frosty the Cupcake

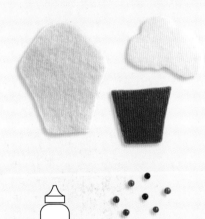

Chip the Cookie

Jolly the Milk Jug

Forest Friends

Create a critter collection inspired by the great outdoors.

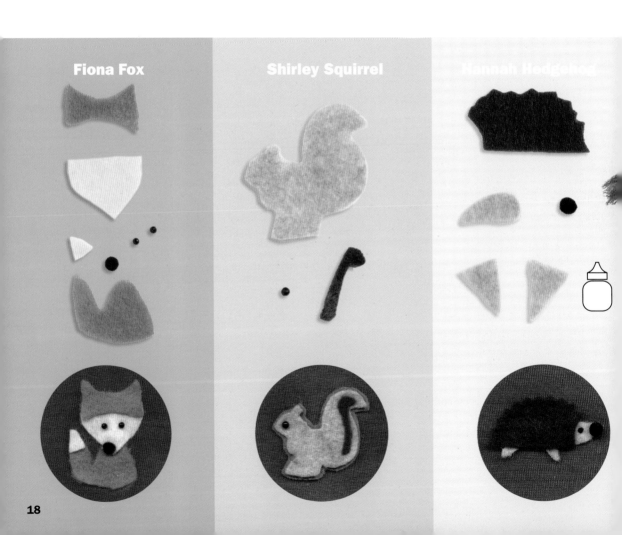

Fiona Fox

Shirley Squirrel

Hannah Hedgehog

Farm Fresh

Veggies and bunnies go together like peas in a pod.

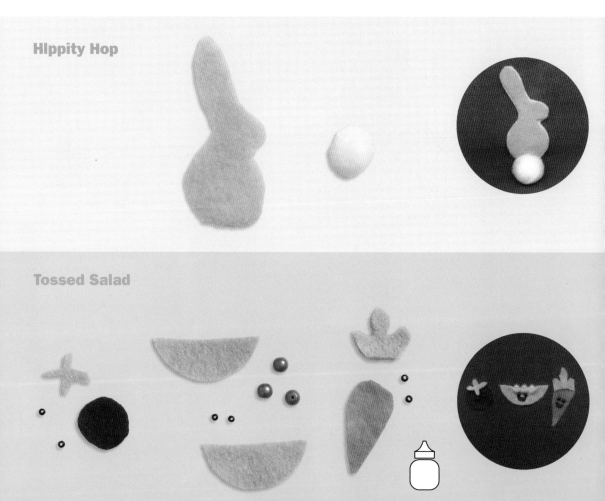

Hippity Hop

Tossed Salad

Beach Buddies

Set your sights on the sea for these tidal tees.

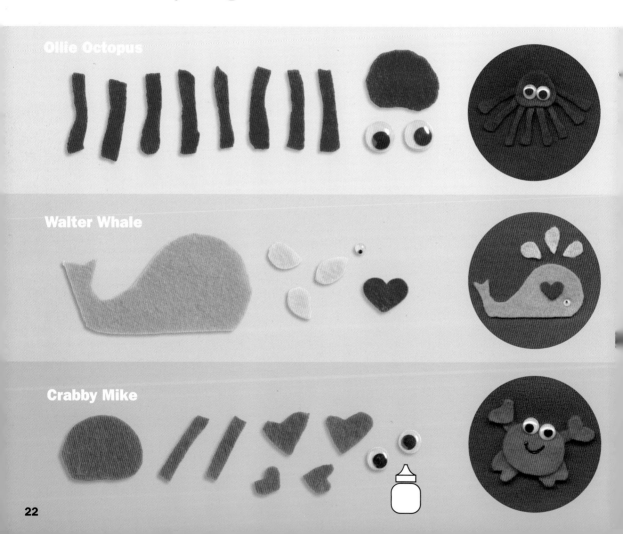

Ollie Octopus

Walter Whale

Crabby Mike

Fruity Cuties

Add flavor to fashion with these fruit friends.

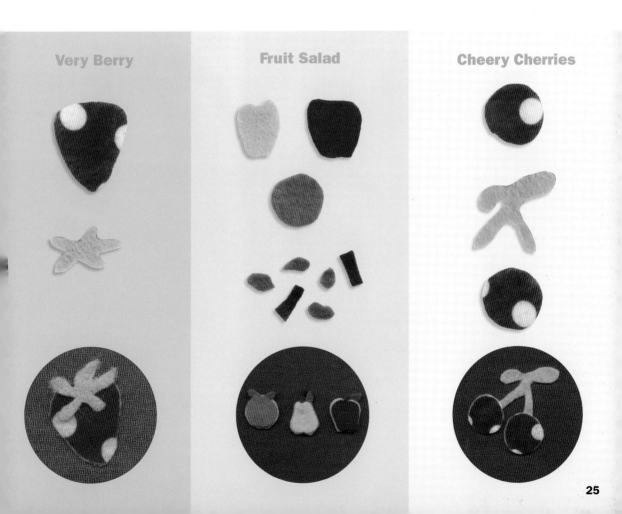

Very Berry

Fruit Salad

Cheery Cherries

Sunny Sal

Stormy Cloud and the Drops

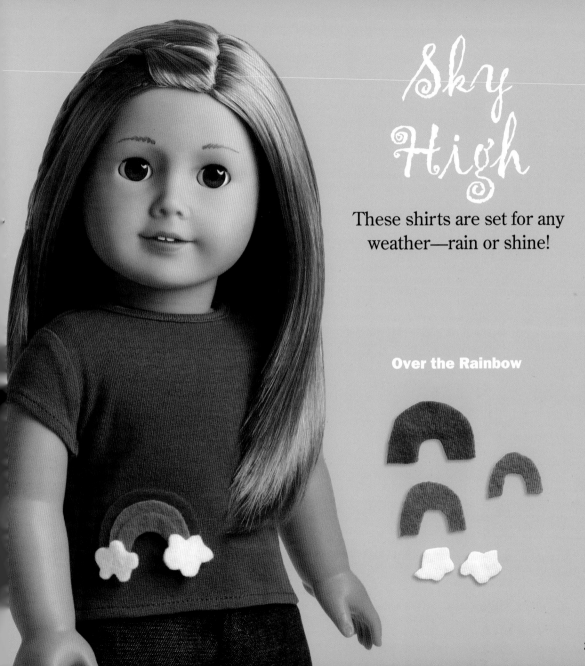

Sky High

These shirts are set for any weather—rain or shine!

Over the Rainbow

Outdoor Outing

Make tees perfect for a picnic in the park.

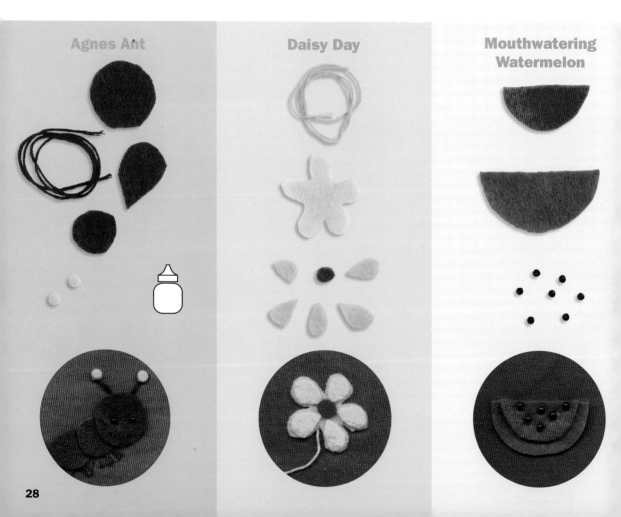

Agnes Ant

Daisy Day

Mouthwatering Watermelon

Alien Invasion

Beam up tees that are out of this world.

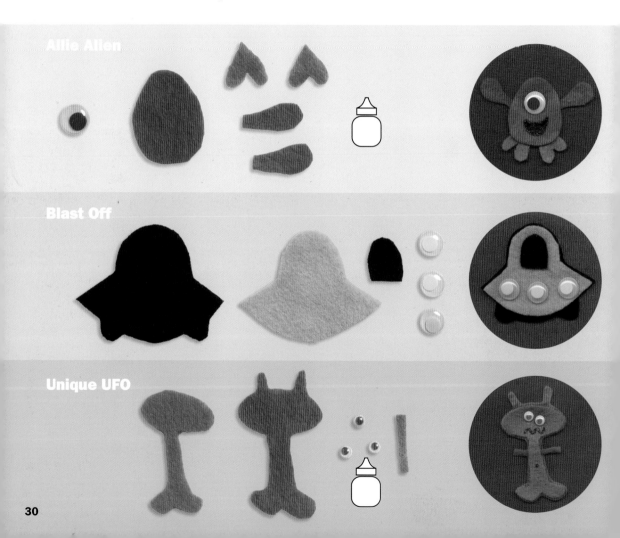

Allie Alien

Blast Off

Unique UFO

Show us
your
styles!

Share a picture of your doll's favorite tee!

Send photo to:

Doll Tees Felt Fashions Editor
American Girl
8400 Fairway Place
Middleton, WI 53562

(Photos can't be returned. All comments
and suggestions received by American Girl
Publishing may be used without
compensation or acknowledgment.)